Show Me the Money

Workbook

Show Me the Money Workbook
Published by Guy Thing Press
P.O. Box 827
Roanoke, TX 76262

This book or parts thereof may not be reproduced in any form, stored in a retrieval system, or transmitted in any form by any means - electronic, mechanical, photocopy, recording, or otherwise - without prior written permission of the publisher, except as provided by United States of America copyright law.

Guy Thing Press books may be purchased in bulk for educational, business, fund-raising, or sales promotional use. For more information, please contact Guy Thing Press.

Please visit us at www.guythingpress.com

Copyright © 2008 by Guy Thing Press
All Rights Reserved

Printed in the United States of America

ISBN-13: 978-0-9818337-3-6
ISBN-10: 0-9818337-3-6

Scripture taken from the New King James Version. Copyright © 1982 by Thomas Nelson, Inc. Used by permission. All rights reserved.

Contents

Chapter One: You Need More Money 1

Chapter Two: The Problem with Poverty 7

Chapter Three: What About the Poor? 13

Chapter Four: A Mind for Money 21

Chapter Five: Is it God's Will for You to Prosper? 29

Chapter Six: Your Financial Attitude Will Determine Your Financial Altitude 35

Chapter Seven: The Love of Money. 41

Chapter Eight: Overcoming Financial Powerlessness 47

Chapter Nine: A Foundation for Debt Cancellation. 53

Chapter Ten: Preparing for Prosperity 59

Chapter Eleven: Things That Sabotage Success 65

Chapter Twelve: Setting the Stage for Success 71

Chapter Thirteen: Making the Journey to Blessing 77

Chapter Fourteen: The Principle of Sowing and Reaping 83

Chapter Fifteen: What Is the Tithe? 87

Chapter Sixteen: The Power of Generosity. 93

Chapter Seventeen: Money Works Generationally. 99

Chapter 1
You Need More Money

Show Me the Money

1. In what way is money a representation of our life?
_____
_____
_____

2. _____ is a term we have transposed in our country to mean money.

3. Our Western culture does not differentiate between _____ and _____.

4. Christ told us not to focus on riches because _____
_____.

5. What words does the bible typically use to define prosperity?
_____
_____

6. Prosperity is the natural, sequentially ordered result of _____.

7. How you spend your money shows what you _____, and is a qualifier for _____. Jesus said that if a man cannot be faithful with _____, he can never qualify for true _____.

8. What does the term "financial freedom" mean?
_____
_____

Chapter 1
You Need More Money

9. God wants to use your _____ to confirm His covenant on the Earth. He wants to use your _____ to create, manufacture, and obtain wealth as a witness and as a tool.

10. Before you were saved, the promise of prosperity was _____ _____. Now, it is evidence of _____.

Show Me the Money

Chapter 1
You Need More Money

Key Point Review

1. Money is a representation of our _____.

2. _____ are something we have. _____ is something we are.

3. Financial freedom isn't about having _____ to do what you want, but having the resources that _____ towards God's calling in your life.

4. Only _____ have the power to control our thoughts.

5. Before you were saved, Christianity was all about _____. Now that you are saved, it is all about _____.

Chapter 2
The Problem With Poverty

Show Me the Money

1. The word "economics" means _____.

2. Proper stewardship of material resources establishes _____ and _____.

3. A poverty mentality has nothing to do with how much money you have, but rather _____.

4. There are five common elements to a poverty world view: _____
_____
_____

5. A _____ is someone who watches over something and cares for it. A _____ accumulates out of fear and even lust.

6. We all have three things to give: Our _____, _____, and _____.

7. People who have a poverty mindset or lack in their spiritual, emotional and mental DNA believe that they are _____.

8. On a fundamental level, it reflects _____.

9. _____ is the greatest obstacle that we will face in fulfilling our destinies and allowing God to let us prosper.

10. A significant part of the poverty mentality is the _____
_____.

Chapter 2
The Problem With Poverty

11. What can an attitude of withholding be likened to?

_____

_____

12. A poverty mind-set, like a prosperous mind-set, is a _____.

Show Me the Money

Chapter 2
The Problem With Poverty

Key Point Review

1. Economics means _____.

2. A Poverty mentality has to do with your _____ toward money.

3. A mind-set is a _____.

4. Being a _____ and being a _____ are two different things.

5. True motivation for a miser mind-set tends to be lack of _____.

6. You can only deal with defective DNA though the process of _____ _____.

7. People with a _____ outlook will not invest in the Kingdom of God.

Chapter 3
What About the Poor?

Show Me the Money

1. Poverty is something we _____ through. It is not something we are supposed to _____ in.

2. What are the four aspects of poverty, as defined in the book?
    _____

3. If having _____ does not make you a man of God, how can being _____ make you a man of God?

4. _____ prosperity is built over a lifetime.

5. Poverty is supposed to be _____. Prosperity is supposed to be _____.

Fill in the tables found on the following pages using the scriptures provided.
(These are the same tables found in your book.)

For Table #1, write the single-word reason for poverty in the column next to the provided scripture.

In Table #2, write the causes for prosperity in the column by the scriptures provided.

Chapter 3
What About the Poor?

TABLE 1 SCRIPTURAL REASONS FOR POVERTY	
Prov 10:4 Lazy hands make a man poor, but diligent hands bring wealth.	
Prov 6:10-11 A little sleep, a little slumber, a little folding of the hands to rest - and **poverty** will come on you like a bandit and scarcity like an armed man.	
Prov 11:24 One man gives freely, yet gains even more; another withholds unduly, but comes to **poverty.**	
Prov 13:18 He who ignores discipline comes to **poverty** and shame, but whoever heeds correction is honored.	
Prov 14:23 All hard work brings a profit, but mere talk leads only to **poverty.**	
Prov 20:13 Do not love sleep or you will grow poor; stay awake and you will have food to spare.	
Prov 21:5 The plans of the diligent lead to profit as surely as haste leads to **poverty.**	
Prov 22:16 He who oppresses the poor to increase his wealth and he who gives gifts to the rich - both come to **poverty.**	
Prov 23:21 for drunkards and gluttons become poor, and drowsiness clothes them in rags.	
Prov 28:19 He who works his land will have abundant food, but the one who chases fantasies will have his fill of **poverty**.	
Prov 28:13 He who conceals his sins does not prosper but whoever confesses and renounces them finds mercy.	
Prov 28:22 A stingy man is eager to get rich and is unaware that **poverty** awaits him.	

TABLE 2 BIBLICAL REASONS FOR PROSPERITY	
Prov 11:25 A generous man will prosper; he who refreshes others will himself be refreshed.	
Prov 28:25 A greedy man stirs up dissension, but he who trusts in the LORD will prosper.	
Ps 1:1-3 Blessed is the man who does not walk in the counsel of the wicked or stand in the way of sinners or sit in the seat of mockers. But his delight is in the law of the LORD, and on his law he meditates day and night. He is like a tree planted by streams of water, which yields its fruit in season and whose leaf does not wither. Whatever he does prospers.	
De 5:33 Walk in all the way that the LORD your God has commanded you, so that you may live and prosper and prolong your days in the land that you will possess.	
De 6:24 The LORD commanded us to obey all these decrees and to fear the LORD our God, so that we might always prosper and be kept alive, as is the case today.	
De 29:9 Carefully follow the terms of this covenant, so that you may prosper in everything you do.	
1Ki 2:3 and observe what the LORD your God requires: Walk in his ways, and keep his decrees and commands, his laws and requirements, as written in the Law of Moses, so that you may prosper in all you do and wherever you go,	
Prov 16:20 Whoever gives heed to instruction prospers, and blessed is he who trusts in the LORD.	
Ec 11:6 Sow your seed in the morning, and at evening let not your hands be idle, for you do not know which will succeed, whether this or that, or whether both will do equally well.	
Ps 122:9 For the sake of the house of the LORD our God, I will seek your **prosperity**.	
Ps 128:2 You will eat the fruit of your labor; blessings and **prosperity** will be yours.	

Chapter 3
What About the Poor?

Prov 8:12-21 I, Wisdom, dwell together with prudence; I possess knowledge and discretion. To fear the LORD is to hate evil; I hate pride and arrogance, evil behavior and perverse speech. Counsel and sound judgment are mine; I have understanding and power. By me kings reign and rulers make laws that are just; by me princes govern, and all nobles who rule on earth. I love those who love me, and those who seek me find me. With me are riches and honor, enduring wealth and **prosperity**. My fruit is better than fine gold; what I yield surpasses choice silver. I walk in the way of righteousness, along the paths of justice bestowing wealth on those who love me and making their treasuries full.	
Prov 13:21 Misfortune pursues the sinner, but **prosperity** is the reward of the righteous.	
Mal 3:8-12 "Will a man rob God? Yet you rob me. But you ask, 'How do we rob you?' In tithes and offerings. You are under a curse - the whole nation of you - because you are robbing me. Bring the whole tithe into the storehouse, that there may be food in my house. Test me in this," says the LORD Almighty, "and see if I will not throw open the floodgates of heaven and pour out so much blessing that you will not have room enough for it. I will prevent pests from devouring your crops, and the vines in your fields will not cast their fruit," says the LORD Almighty. "Then all the nations will call you blessed, for yours will be a delightful land," says the LORD Almighty.	
Prov 21:21 He who pursues righteousness and love finds life, **prosperity** and honor.	

Show Me the Money

Show Me the Money

Chapter 3
What About the Poor?

Key Point Review

1. Using the scriptures from the first table, reflect on what you have read and how it applies to you personally. List the five areas from the Word that you think may be a cause of poverty or lack in your life.

- _____
- _____
- _____
- _____
- _____

2. Using the second table, list five reasons you think you should be prospering.

- _____
- _____
- _____
- _____
- _____

Chapter 4
A Mind for Money

Show Me the Money

1. Why is your perception so important?
   _____
   _____
   _____

2. What must we do in order to see positive change in our finances?
   _____
   _____
   _____

3. _____ is negative; _____ is positive.

4. The thing that brings freedom is _____.

5. All truth starts as _____. It must then become _____.

6. Before a revelation can become a _____, it must be applied.

7. To _____ means to renovate or change for the better.

8. What are the four levels of thinking described in 2 Corinthians 2:3-5?
   _____
   _____

Show Me the Money

Chapter 4
A Mind for Money

9. Thoughts are described as _____ and _____.

10. Your thoughts are the past _____ of the _____ you currently live in.

11. Arguments are reasons and opinions based on _____.

Show Me the Money

Chapter 4
A Mind for Money

Key Point Review

1. God is _____ and he never builds on the _____.

2. Information has to be _____. It has to move from being _____ to _____.

3. What can renewing your mind do in your life?
   _____
   _____

4. Thoughts are the _____ of your soul today.

5. Thoughts of the future are the _____ of your destiny.

Chapter 5
Is it God's Will for You to Prosper?

Show Me the Money

1. According to Deuteronomy 8:17, what can we infer about God's desire for us to prosper?
   _____
   _____
   _____

2. We are called to be _____ of all that God has created.

3. If God doesn't want you to have wealth, why did he give you the power to get it?
   _____
   _____
   _____

4. Why did He promise prosperity and success if He prefers us to remain poor?
   _____
   _____
   _____

5. If God does not want us to prosper, why did he tell us that reading his word day and night would lead to prosperity and success?
   _____
   _____
   _____

6. Why did He tell us that the wealth of the wicked, the unrighteous, and those who don't follow and love Him, is being held until we collect it?
   _____
   _____
   _____

Chapter 5
Is It God's Will for You to Prosper?

7. Financial wealth is only one aspect of personal _____.

8. To deny God's prosperity is to deny the _____ and _____ that He wants to bestow on us.

9. Financial prosperity is not an excuse to justify your _____, _____ lifestyle.

Show Me the Money

Chapter 5
Is It God's Will for You to Prosper?

Key Point Review

1. Does God want you to prosper? _____

2. What are some scriptures that show this desire God has toward our lives?
   _____
   _____

3. God provides through _____.

4. According to the book, what is prosperity *not* considered to be?
   _____
   _____
   _____

5. Why does God want you to prosper?
   _____

Show Me the Money

Chapter 6
Your Financial Attitude Will Determine Your Financial Altitude

Show Me the Money

1. What, according to the author, robs people of the blessing God has for them?
   _____

2. You have the _____, but you need to get practical. It takes _____ to pay the bills, feed the poor, and start a ministry.

3. One of the enemy's greatest tactics is to _____
   _____
   _?

4. According to Dr. John Binkley, what has been one of the reasons why the earth has not been covered with the glory of God?
   _____
   _____
   _____

5. Why has Satan been trying to plant doubt in us concerning this area?
   _____
   _____
   _____

6. Why is it self-centered to think you don't need money?
   _____
   _____
   _____

Chapter 6
Your Financial Attitude Will Determine Your Financial Altitude

7. Money says to land "_____."
   Money says to vision "_____."
   Money says to buildings "_____."
   Money says to a missionary "_____."
   Money says to things "_____."
   Money says to poverty "_____."
   Money says to opportunity "_____."

8. How does money have the ability to facilitate the establishment of the Kingdom?
   _____
   _____
   _____

Show Me the Money

Show Me the Money

Chapter 6
Your Financial Attitude Will Determine Your Financial Altitude

Key Point Review

1. You do not _____ the things you have, but you are only a _____ of them.

2. One of the enemy's greatest tactics is to stop God's people from having _____
_____.

3. You have to learn to see and think beyond your own _____ to see the real power of money.

4. Resist the kind of thinking that limits your life and finances to having _____
_____.

Show Me the Money

Show Me the Money

Chapter 7
The Love of Money

Show Me the Money

1. If you accept another person's philosophies that are really a _____ or _____ for their failure, then in reality, their failure becomes yours.

2. What three scriptures give people the most challenge concerning money?
   _____

3. If you do not have the resources, you are _____, a point of brokenness, in a way that few people of wealth ever know.

4. What did Christ say specifically about a person of financial substance entering the kingdom?
   _____
   _____
   _____

5. Define the term "serve."
   _____
   _____

6. The issue isn't money in the scriptures; it is _____ and _____. It is the issue of _____.

7. The focus or issue of Matthew 6:24 is not money, but _____.

8. When money is not worshipped, it is seen as a _____ and not an _____.

Chapter 7
The Love of Money

9. How do you ensure that you don't fall in to the Love-Money Trap?

_____

_____

_____

10. What are the signs of a God-sized vision and a God-inspired life?

_____

_____

_____

_____

Show Me the Money

Chapter 7
The Love of Money

Key Point Review

Answer the following questions with honesty.

1. Do you react negatively to the thought or mention of giving, or offerings?
   _____
   _____
   _____

2. Do you resent what other people have?
   _____
   _____
   _____

3. Are you living in a moral "gray zone?"
   _____
   _____
   _____

4. Are you tight-fisted or a good steward?
   _____
   _____
   _____

5. Is money too high on your agenda?
   _____
   _____
   _____

Show Me the Money

Chapter 8
Overcoming Financial Powerlessness

Show Me the Money

1. Life is arrived at in _____, but it is lived on _____.

2. Circumstances do not determine your destiny, _____ do.

3. Why do we become slaves to our choices?
   _____
   _____
   _____

4. What happens when you refuse to choose?
   _____
   _____

5. Everything in the Bible is done according to a pattern that is _____
   _____.

6. The Bible teaches that, along with wisdom, we are to _____.

7. What is the difference between knowledge and understanding?
   _____
   _____
   _____

8. Deuteronomy 8:18 doesn't say that God _____ you wealth, but gives you the power to _____ wealth.

Chapter 8
Overcoming Financial Powerlessness

9. What 7 biblical principles are the foundations of your financial freedom and prosperity?

_____
_____
_____

10. How is unemployment like a cancer to a man's soul?

_____
_____
_____

Show Me the Money

Chapter 8
Overcoming Financial Powerlessness

Key Point Review

1. _____ do not determine your destiny, your _____.

2. All truth is parallel. What works in the Kingdom of God works in the Kingdom of _____.

3. God does not want to get something from you, but wants to _____ _____.

4. After reading the chapter, can you say you have been living within your means?
   _____
   _____
   _____

5. What changes can you make to overcome your financial powerlessness?
   _____
   _____
   _____

Chapter 9
A Foundation for Debt Cancellation

Show Me the Money

1. The average family spends about _____ of its disposable income on debt repayment.

2. Jesus did not die to save you from your _____, but from your _____.

3. Don't pray for a miracle, _____.

4. Getting out of debt involves much more than just wishing, hoping, and praying for it to happen. Getting there and staying there involves _____.

5. What are the three things you can do to get rid of your debt?
   _____

6. What is involved with changing your mind-set?
   _____
   _____
   _____

7. What is involved in paying your tithes?
   _____
   _____
   _____

8. What is involved in paying yourself?
   _____
   _____
   _____

Show Me the Money

Chapter 9
A Foundation for Debt Cancellation

9. How much should you put into your savings account every month?
_____

10. As an alternative to 10%, what can you do to save if you aren't able to set aside 10%?
_____
_____
_____

Show Me the Money

Show Me the Money

Chapter 9
A Foundation for Debt Cancellation

Key Point Review

1. How has the financial mind-set in America changed since World War II?
   _____
   _____
   _____

2. How can debt strangle you and God's plans for you?
   _____
   _____
   _____

3. How does bringing the tithe into the storehouse benefit us in reducing our debt?
   _____
   _____
   _____

Show Me the Money

Chapter 10
Preparing for Prosperity

Show Me the Money

1. _____ will touch every aspect of your life.

2. Prosperity is not a place you arrive at, but _____.

3. What should you do in times that you don't feel prosperous?
   _____
   _____
   _____

4. In what time frame are the promises of God proven to us?
   _____
   _____

5. What are the five key components to SMART goals?
   _____

6. Acquiring new levels requires a change in _____, _____, and _____.

7. According to Albert Einstein, what is the definition of insanity?
   _____
   _____

8. You must get a revelation that God takes pleasure in the _____ of his people, and you must actively build your _____ and _____ as a child of God, based on the Word of God.

Chapter 10
Preparing for Prosperity

9. If you want the Lord to give you the power to get wealth, it's going to take _____.

10. How are faith and fear similar?
_____
_____

11. Your _____ will take you places your _____ can't sustain you.

12. Why should you acknowledge God when you prosper?
_____
_____

Show Me the Money

**Chapter 10
Preparing for Prosperity**

Key Point Review

1. _____ is not a place you arrive at, but a place you journey to.

2. What are the twelve things that can play a role in helping you prepare for prosperity?
   _____
   _____
   _____

Show Me the Money

Show Me the Money

Chapter 11
Things That Sabotage Success

Show Me the Money

1. And inheritance quickly or untimely gained _____.

2. The true sign of maturity lies not in a man's age, but in _____ _____.

3. Focus on the fulfillment of _____. Postpone the pursuit of _____ until a more suitable time.

4. How should we view failure?
   _____
   _____

5. Why should we not allow chaos to rule our lives?
   _____
   _____

6. _____ is the seed of our success, _____ is the fuel to our success, _____ ensures our success.

7. When do people generally tend to get discouraged?
   _____
   _____

8. Leadership is best defined as _____.

9. What makes up your personal capital?
   _____

Chapter 11
Things That Sabotage Success

10. Why is listening important in being successful?
    _____
    _____

11. What does mediocrity mean?
    _____
    _____

12. What does religion mean?
    _____
    _____

13. Where does the prosperity of a nation, organization, or family lie?
    _____

Show Me the Money

Show Me the Money

Chapter 11
Things That Sabotage Success

Key Point Review

1. An inheritance quickly gained is _____.

2. What are the 14 common traits found in people who sabotage their success?
   _____
   _____
   _____

3. What does the acronym for FEAR stand for, as defined by the book?
   F_____
   E_____
   A_____
   R_____

Show Me the Money

Chapter 12
Setting the Stage for Success

Show Me the Money

1. How have people come to equate Godliness with prosperity?
   _____
   _____
   _____

2. The more God blesses you, the greater _____
   _____.

3. Define Stewardship.
   _____
   _____

4. What are the six factors for setting the stage for your success?
   _____
   _____

5. What are the "Big Three?"
   _____

6. Why is being rich not the goal?
   _____
   _____

7. Make sure you are pursuing the _____, not the _____.

Chapter 12
Setting the Stage for Success

Show Me the Money

Chapter 12
Setting the Stage for Success

Key Point Review

1. Stewardship is more than making _____.

2. When does profit come in the Christian's life?
   _____
   _____

3. Make a distinction between _____ and _____.

4. What colors the morality of your money?
   _____

Show Me the Money

Chapter 13
Making the Journey to Blessing

Show Me the Money

1. What were the five stages the children of Israel had to go through on their journey to the promise?
   _____
   _____
   _____

2. God led the Israelites out of Egypt and into the desert to _____
   _____.

3. Why does God put us through times of "just enough" on our journey to prosperity?
   _____
   _____

4. He gives us the power to have more than enough, but your seed of _____ will not grow if you don't use your _____ to stretch yourself beyond your past limitations.

5. What usually blinds people to their need for God?
   _____
   _____

6. According to Deuteronomy 8:18, how does God get money to us?
   _____
   _____

7. For you to become who you are supposed to become, at some stage you are going to have to ____
   _____, if they are not prepared to grow and change with you.

Chapter 13
Making the Journey to Blessing

8.   Not everyone is called to _____ with you forever.

9.   Relationships should always be _____ but never seen as _____ _____. Love people and their _____ while you travel together, but realize that no one is going to the same destination you are.

Show Me the Money

Show Me the Money

Chapter 13
Making the Journey to Blessing

Key Point Review

1. There are many stages to _____.

2. Our times of "just enough" are meant to refine our _____.

3. God is often revealed to us in _____.

4. God doesn't give you money, but rather _____.

Show Me the Money

Chapter 14
The Principle of Sowing and Reaping

Show Me the Money

1. When you live according to the powerful principles of the Word, _____
   _____
   _____.

2. Every action or decision has _____.

3. What are the principles of sowing and reaping dependent on?
   _____

4. The principles of sowing and reaping are much more than simply principles of money; they are
   _____.

5. What are the three things we can sow?
   _____

6. In what way does God give back our tithe?
   _____
   _____
   _____

7. You can not _____ or _____ the grace of God.

8. How do you know when you are sowing to the flesh?
   _____

9. How do you know when you are sowing to the Spirit?
   _____

Chapter 14
The Principle of Sowing and Reaping

Show Me the Money

Chapter 14
The Principle of Sowing and Reaping

Key Point Review

1. Every action or decision has a _____.

2. If you sow, you have to be prepared to _____.

3. Sowing to the flesh is motivated by a _____ attitude.

4. You cannot get the things of God through the _____.

Show Me the Money

Show Me the Money

Chapter 15
What Is the Tithe?

Show Me the Money

1. What is the significance of the tithe?
   _____
   _____
   _____

2. From creation, God established the principle of first fruits and the tithe _____ _____ _____ of good men.

3. What did Jesus teach regarding taxation?
   _____
   _____

4. What did Jesus teach regarding offerings?
   _____

5. On a practical level, tithing is all about _____
   _____.

6. The principle of first fruits and _____ is your choice.

7. Is it better to tithe before or after taxes? Why?
   _____
   _____
   _____

8. Rather than making tithing an issue of rigid law, what should we make it an issue of?
   _____
   _____
   _____

Chapter 15
What Is the Tithe?

9. Where should you put your tithe?
_____
_____

Chapter 15
What Is the Tithe?

Show Me the Money

Show Me the Money

Chapter 15
What Is the Tithe?

Key Point Review

1. The tithe means _____ of the gross income.

2. From creation, God established the principle of first fruits and the tithe _____ _____ _____ of good men.

3. Tithing _____ the law and was not eradicated by Christ of the Apostles in the New Testament.

4. Jesus didn't say things would be added to you just because _____. He said you must put the _____ first.

5. Tithing is an issue of the _____.

Show Me the Money

Chapter 16
The Power of Generosity

Show Me the Money

1. _____ is a spirit that affects your thinking, your decisions, and everything about your life.

2. True generosity isn't measured by the _____.

3. A spirit of generosity cannot be proven in a single act, but rather is proven in _____.

4. Write Proverbs 11:24-25
   _____
   _____
   _____

5. Generosity has the ability to make you _____ on the inside.

6. A generous soul will see people and situations in a _____ light.

7. If you are always looking for a _____-_____, then you will always be _____.

8. People who hold onto their possessions won't get _____, but if a generous spirit gives liberally, there is _____.

9. What five things will help you become a more generous person?
   _____
   _____

Chapter 16
The Power of Generosity

Show Me the Money

Chapter 16
The Power of Generosity

Key Point Review

1. _____ does not relate to how much you have, because a _____ _____ operates under any circumstance.

2. Generosity has the ability to make you _____ on the inside.

3. The power of having a generous spirit puts you in a position to _____ _____ _____.

4. Generosity is a way of _____. It is not empty words of _____, but words that speak _____.

5. Generosity is not about what you are going to _____.

Show Me the Money

Chapter 17
Money Works Generationally

Show Me the Money

1. The choices we make today have the power to _____ _____.

2. If you want to change your _____ and begin to build godly foundations for future generations, your approach to _____ is the key.

3. What is God's pipeline for blessing?
   _____

4. What did God tell Abraham was central to his walk in the power of God's covenant?
   _____
   _____
   _____

5. What does God require us to do with our wealth?
   _____
   _____

6. _____ are an inheritance from the Lord whom we are given the responsibility to steward. We must _____ for them, _____ for them, and _____ for them.

7. How do you build an inheritance for your children?
   _____

8. What are the three elements that form the backbone of creating a generational inheritance?
   _____
   _____

Chapter 17
Money Works Generationally

9. What is the best inheritance to leave your children?

_____

_____

Show Me the Money

Chapter 17
Money Works Generationally

Key Point Review

1. Family members impart to one another things that are _____ and _____.

2. Your approach to _____ is the key to building a Godly foundation and inheritance.

3. The _____ is the basic wealth-generating unit of the Bible.

4. After reading the chapter, what areas can you change and build upon to insure that your children are receiving an appropriate inheritance from you?

_____
_____
_____
_____
_____
_____

Show Me the Money

Show Me the Money

Resources of Interest

Character is King
Dr. John Binkley

It's a Guy Thing: Character is King takes you on your dream journey. There is a place called destiny that we all journey to. We all have ideas, dreams and vision for what life should be. This book lays out a plan for that journey to realizing your dreams, and to your destiny.

Let's Talk About Sex
Dr. John A. King

Let's face it. Sexuality is all around us. It's even on billboards, magazines and television commercials. Sadly, It's a topic many men and women have to deal with on their own because too many churches or pastors won't touch it. Find out what the Bible has to say about some of the toughest questions in *Let's Talk About Sex*.

Now to Next
Dr. John A. King

What does the next generation church look like? Who are the people that will be involved in the next generation church? How will it come about?

Those are some of the questions answered in Dr. King's newest release, *Now to Next: Blueprint for a Christian Revolution*.

Helping Guys Become Men, Husbands, and Fathers
Dr. John A. King

It's a Guy Thing takes you on the journey of fatherhood. Dr. John King shares the skills necessary to become a good father. He shows you what can happen when a father is absent or simply not active in a child's life. Being a male is a matter of birth. Being a man is a matter of choice. This book will help you make that choice.

To see all the titles available through Guy Thing Press, visit us online at www.guythingpress.com

Resources of Interest

Business By The Book
Dr. John A. King

The world's greatest handbook on leadership, economic and social excellence is not found in schoolbooks, but in Scripture. The principles in this book are tried, proven and resilient over centuries. Christ bet His life on it, and so can you.

Show Me the Money
Dr. John A. King

Time Magazine asked, "Does God want you to be rich?" The answer to that question is simply "No, God wants you to be *wealthy*." In *Show Me the Money*, you will learn the fundamentals of creating and using wealth in God's kingdom.

Achieving Authentic Wealth
Jeff McLoud

We need a vision that goes beyond our ability to be consumers only. A vision so big, so powerful, that we cannot even accomplish it in our own lifetime - a vision founded from the very heartbeat of God. We could see the vision fulfilled if we ask ourselves a simple question: "How can we achieve twice as much with half the money?"

Creating a Better Life
Erik A. Kudlis

In this easy to read manual, educator and administrator turned international businessman, Erik Kudlis, identifies three vital keys you must know and use, given by God Himself, that unlock the doors to the life God has always wanted you to have.

To see all the titles available through Guy Thing Press, visit us online at www.guythingpress.com

Further Resources

The Godly Man Curriculum

The Godly Man Curriculum is designed to train men from all walks of life, giving them a firm foundation of doctrine and Godly knowledge. This curriculum is available both over the internet for individual study and on DVD for seminars, Sunday schools, and men's meetings. With up to 7 hours of video teaching divided over numerous topics, the Godly Man Curriculum is an excellent tool that you can build your classes upon and grow yourself and your people.

Listen to sample teachings from the Godly Man Curriculum at www.imnonline.org.

Building Iron Men & Life As Leaders Networks

The Building Iron Men and Life as Leaders networks are two of IMN's finest resources. Each network provides you with a new teaching every month that will challenge and encourage you to grow. The Building Iron Men network features three teachings in both CD and DVD format that are tailored for men, while the Life as Leaders network provides you with three CDs that teach leadership principles anyone can use.

Both networks are phenomenal tools that are vital assets to any church and discipleship program.

Also check out these websites for great resources and training materials.

International Men's Network
www.imnonline.org

Guy Thing Press
www.guythingpress.com

IMN
INTERNATIONAL MEN'S NETWORK

The International Men's Network was founded by Dr. John A. King. Its purpose is to help men grow to become the leaders their families and churches need and become men of God that make a lasting impact on those around them.

IMN is a missionary organization to the men of the world. We are committed to:

- Inspire all men to rise to a high standard of biblical manhood.
- Encourage them to excel in their roles as men, leaders, husbands, and fathers.
- Challenge them to be contributors to society and set an example based upon a biblical value system that will benefit this generation and lay a solid foundation for the next generation.

The International Men's Network is dedicated to providing and hosting the best resources for men, including teachings and lessons on CD and DVD and conferences that teach men the principles that will help them become more influential and effective in their lives.

For more information about IMN and its mission, visit us online at www.imnonline.org or call 817.993.0047

The Christian Life Center was founded by Dr. John King and his wife, Beccy. With a vision to preach the gospel of Jesus Christ with unashamed passion and uncompromising truth, Christian Life Center aims to raise up the next generation of leaders to move into all the world and proclaim the truth of Christ to the lost and broken.

Located in the Keller, Texas area, the church sits in the prime location to reach the community and the people therein. The church desires to give back to the community by providing outreaches to better and enrich its inhabitants. From kickboxing classes that are aimed at teaching children and adults self-defense, to a special service that commemorates and honors our country's war-time heroes, Christian Life Center strives to bring a living Jesus to a dying world by new and imaginative means that will bless and change lives.

For more information about Christian Life Center and the resources it offers, visit the website at www.clctx.org

www.ingramcontent.com/pod-product-compliance
Lightning Source LLC
LaVergne TN
LVHW081539060526
838200LV00048B/2142